OVERCOMING

PHYSICAL

DEATH

Jesus taught and demonstrated
the Overcoming of Physical Death.
--AND--
In John 14:12 Jesus said that
we would do the things he did.

Mel Sperber

© Copyright 2005 Mel Sperber
All rights reserved. No part of this publication may be reproduced, stored in a retrieval system, or transmitted, in any form or by any means, electronic, mechanical, photocopying, recording, or otherwise, without the written prior permission of the author.

Note for Librarians: a cataloguing record for this book that includes Dewey Decimal Classification and US Library of Congress numbers is available from the Library and Archives of Canada. The complete cataloguing record can be obtained from their online database at:
www.collectionscanada.ca/amicus/index-e.html
ISBN 1-4120-5081-2
Printed in Victoria, BC, Canada

TRAFFORD

Offices in Canada, USA, Ireland, UK and Spain
This book was published *on-demand* in cooperation with Trafford Publishing. On-demand publishing is a unique process and service of making a book available for retail sale to the public taking advantage of on-demand manufacturing and Internet marketing. On-demand publishing includes promotions, retail sales, manufacturing, order fulfilment, accounting and collecting royalties on behalf of the author.

Book sales for North America and international:
Trafford Publishing, 6E–2333 Government St.,
Victoria, BC V8T 4P4 CANADA
phone 250 383 6864 (toll-free 1 888 232 4444)
fax 250 383 6804; email to orders@trafford.com
Book sales in Europe:
Trafford Publishing (UK) Ltd., Enterprise House, Wistaston Road Business Centre,
Wistaston Road, Crewe, Cheshire CW2 7RP UNITED KINGDOM
phone 01270 251 396 (local rate 0845 230 9601)
facsimile 01270 254 983; orders.uk@trafford.com
Order online at:
www.trafford.com/robots/04-2889.html

10 9 8 7 6 5 4 3

Table of Contents

Introduction

Jesus taught and demonstrated the Overcoming of Physical Death, and in John 14:12 He said that we would do the things that He did.

Also, in John 8:51 Jesus said: "If a man keep my saying, he shall never see death".

And, in I Cor 15:26 Paul states: "The last enemy that shall be destroyed is death".

Man is a spiritual being, a soul, who already has Eternal Life, but the Divine Plan was for man (a Spiritual Being) to temporarily have a physical experience in a physical body.

During this period he was to develop certain spiritual qualities after which he would no longer need a physical body and would eliminate it permanently.

Unfortunately, he failed to develop as intended, and man became trapped in a physical body, and continues to undergo round after round of physical death and physical rebirth through a process of reincarnation.

1

There is a simple and effective way of fulfilling Jesus' call for conquering the last enemy, physical death, even as Jesus did.

What follows provides the information necessary to make this possible.

Instructions

The Life and Teachings of Jesus, as well as other Avatars before Him, leave no doubt that our ultimate goal while on this earth is to develop Spiritually, attain Perfection in every way, and achieve Eternal Life, making Reincarnation no longer necessary and opening the way for further Evolution of Consciousness.

The contents of this booklet, if seriously put into practice, will help considerably toward accomplishing that end.

In order to avoid any misunderstanding, and fully comprehend and benefit from this material, it should be read from beginning to end very carefully as often as possible.

The meditation should be read during your meditation time a number of times each day while in a very relaxed state. As soon as possible, however, the meditation should be memorized.

Special attention should be given to the Violet Fire since it's the Negative Energy that's causing the problem.

3

The Ascended Masters

God looks after the World with the help of beings who once lived on Earth as human beings. They developed spiritually to such an extent that they were able to ascend into their God-Selves, even as Jesus did. There are thousands of these beings in the Spiritual Realm.

They are no longer required to return to Earth. In a sense you could say that they graduated from the schoolroom called Earth, and are now considered to be Ascended Masters.

There were certain Ascended Masters who were Avatars, such as Buddha, Moses, Krishna, and Jesus himself, who entered the scene with a special message from God meant for a particular time and for a particular place. That's how different world religions came into existence.

However, all of the Ascended Masters continue to serve mankind from this Spiritual Realm even today, helping the people of Earth to graduate as they did. Basic to them all is that we should look for God within ourselves rather than somewhere out there.

From time to time the Ascended Masters train someone on Earth who will be able to receive dictations from them, dictations which contain valuable information. This valuable information has been placed in book form, and much of the material in this booklet is based on the teachings therein.

There are many who claim to be channels of those Ascended Masters, but the Ascended Masters say that only those who have been trained by an Ascended Master to receive the messages will be able to channel the whole and absolute Truth.

According to those Ascended Masters, civilization at this time is at a very critical juncture, and time is short. Therefore, it is essential for those of us on Earth today to achieve this so-called graduation as soon as possible.

The Nature of Man

If you were able to live a happy, harmonious life during which you never grew old, you never got sick, and all your needs were card for, I'm sure you wouldn't mind living forever.

However, you might be surprised to learn that whether you're happy or not right now, you already have Eternal Life.

It is said that man is a Spiritual Being.
What makes us Spiritual Beings?

Although human beings consist of Body, Soul, and Spirit, man is basically a Soul, and what is a Soul?

Soul is Total Consciousness.
That's what makes us Spiritual Beings.
And since Consciousness is Eternal and never dies, human beings already have Eternal Life.

Consciousness can live in a physical body.
Consciousness can live in a spiritual body.

6

The consciousness of each human being on earth right now is having a physical experience in a physical body.

The Fall of Man

When man was first created, he was God-Conscious.
All he knew was God, Goodness and Perfection,
and he lived a perfect, happy, joyous life.

He never grew old and he never got sick.
Having been created in God's image, man was a creator,
and all his needs were cared for through a process of
Mental Precipitation.
That was the Garden of Eden of the Bible.

The Divine Plan was for man to live through seven
different periods of time, each period in a different
physical body.
During these periods, he would develop certain God
virtues and become master of energy and vibration on a
lower vibratory level.
At the end of the seven periods of time, he would
automatically ascend, just as Jesus did.

For a while, the ascensions took place successfully.
However, along the way the Divine Plan was interrupted
by the well-known "Fall of Man".

8

Mankind started to experience negative emotions such as hate, fear, worry, anger, and resentment, and a change in Consciousness took place.
The God-Consciousness of Goodness and Perfection developed into a Human-Consciousness of Good and Evil.

As a result, man was no longer able to ascend, and became trapped in a physical body.

The Ascension

Most people, when they hear the phrase "Overcoming
Physical Death", assume that it means keeping the
present physical body alive forever.
But that's not so.
You overcome physical death by no longer having a
physical body — and--no longer experiencing
physical death.
Until then you keep dying and coming back again and
again in another physical body.

Jesus overcame physical death by no longer having a
physical body — and--now lives in a spiritual body,
an I AM or God body, a Body of Light.

He allowed himself to be crucified so that he could
demonstrate the process of overcoming physical
death and achieving Eternal Life.

In Jesus' day, to be eligible for the ascension, you had to
purify your body 100%, and that's what Jesus did.
He completely purified his body as well as his
consciousness, and when he allowed himself to be

crucified, he was telling us that death is one of the steps necessary to achieve Eternal Life.

Technically, though, there is no such thing as death because Consciousness is Eternal.
All that death amounts to is a change of bodies --and-- in almost every case when a person dies, the physical body is changed into another physical body through the process of reincarnation.

After Jesus died and was buried, he came out of the tomb in his Christ body, never again to change into another physical body.
Since his physical body was already 100% purified, it had returned to the Universal Substance and nothing was left behind.

When people die today, the consciousness is transferred from the physical body into the Etheric Body (one of the spiritual bodies).

After a period of rest in the spiritual realm, the consciousness returns to earth to occupy another physical body.

This constant changing of physical bodies goes on and on until we learn what has to be done to change into the Christ body, like Jesus did, and finally to ascend into the permanent I AM or God body and into Eternal Life.

When that happens, we will no longer experience physical death.

Fortunately, due to the short duration of time before certain catastrophic Earth changes are expected to occur, the requirements for the ascension have been eased quite a bit since Jesus walked the earth.

Today, to be eligible for the ascension, the physical body only has to be purified more than 50%.

And when the person dies, his consciousness is transferred into his Etheric Body --and-- he leaves his physical body behind to be cremated after three days, which helps in the purification process.

During the three days, purification of the Etheric Body is completed, and the consciousness is then able to be transferred into the Christ body, then on to the ascension .

12

Overcoming Physical Death

Rarely mentioned, but touched upon throughout
Religious Literature is the topic of overcoming
death and achieving Eternal Life.
In the Bible itself are numerous references to doing away
with dying and attaining Life Everlasting.

For instance:

In John 3:16 Jesus states "God so loved the world that he
gave his only begotten Son that whosoever
believeth in him should not perish but have
Everlasting Life".

In John 2:25 John states "This is the promise that he
promised us, Eternal Life".

In John 3:36 Jesus states "He that believeth on the Son
hath Everlasting Life".
(the Son = the Indwelling I AM)

In John 17:3 Jesus states "This is Life Eternal that they
know thee, the only true God".

In John 11:26 Jesus states "Whosoever liveth and
believeth in me shall never die".
(me – the Indwelling I AM)

In John 8:51 Jesus states "If a man keep my saying, he shall never see death".

In I Cor 15:26 Paul states "The last enemy that shall be destroyed is death".

In I Cor 15:53 Paul states "This mortal must put on immortality".

In II Timothy 1:10 Paul states "Jesus Christ has abolished death, and has brought immortality to light through the gospel".

In I Cor 15:54 Paul states "When the corruptible has put on incorruption, death will be swallowed up in victory".

In Revelation 3:12 it states "He that overcometh shall go out no more".

In John 2:19 Jesus states "Destroy this temple and in three days I will raise it up". (I = the Indwelling I AM)

In John 10:18 Jesus states "I have the power to lay it down, and I have the power to take it up again".

In Romans 6:23 Paul states "The gift of God is Eternal Life".

In I John 2:17 John states "He that doeth the Will of God abideth forever".

As you know, human beings consist of Body, Soul, and Spirit--and--since the Soul and the Spirit already have Eternal Life and continue to live under any and all circumstances, when Jesus or any part of the Bible refers to abolishing death, or never dying, or achieving Eternal Life or immortality, it can only be referring to the physical body since it is only the physical body that can die.

In one short sentence, the Bible provides us with the cause of death.
In Roman 6:23 Paul stated "The wages of sin is death".
What is sin?
Sin is negative thinking, negative feeling, negative speaking, and negative behavior.

God is often given a number of different names, such as Mind, Spirit, Love, Wisdom, and Power, Life, Substance, and so forth.

Another very important name is Energy, Intelligent Energy.
God is Energy -- all around us as well as within us.

Whenever we think or speak or act, especially with strong feeling, we qualify this Energy either positively or negatively and points in between depending upon the specific aspect of Love or Hate.

Therefore, as a result of Negative thinking, feeling, speaking, or behavior (which is responsible for the continuous loss of the physical body again and again life after life), we continue to accumulate Negative Energy.

An important factor that is closely related to Energy is that the physical body vibrates at a certain speed or rate or frequency.

Negative Energy causes the vibratory frequency to slow down.

As the vibratory frequency decreases, the condition of the body worsens and becomes more dense until the frequency slows down to such an extent that the body dies.

In order to stop the continuous loss of the physical body, Negative Energy, which has been accumulated in present and past lives and which is slowing down the rate of vibration of the body, has to be redeemed, purified, perfected, forgiven.

As the Negative Energy is purified, the vibratory rate of the body increases.

As a result, the condition of the body improves and becomes more Spiritual until it reaches such a high vibratory rate that it is completely spiritualized and merges with the Christ Self, and death is overcome.

When Jesus ascended, what used to be his physical body was at that time vibrating at the speed of light, and was completely spiritualized, was a Body of Light.

In addition to redeeming the Negative Energy already accumulated, we have to avoid accumulating more Negative Energy.

The obvious solution is to keep our thoughts, feelings, words, and actions, positive at all times -- seeing only God, Goodness and Perfection, regardless of appearances.

In addition, practicing Unconditional Love should help tremendously.

No doubt Jesus had Unconditional Love in mind when he said in Luke 10:27 "Thou shalt love the Lord thy God with all thy heart, soul, and strength, and thy neighbor as thyself".

As for redeeming the Negative Energy already accumulated, a number of steps will help.

In Galatians 6:7 Paul "As a man soweth, so shall he reap". When you reap what you have sown, you redeem the Negative Energy you have accumulated as a result. However, having accumulated so much Negative Energy in many, many past lives, only a fraction of that total Negative Energy will be redeemed.

Doing Good, while of immense value, will likewise be able to redeem only a small portion of the accumulations.

As you forgive, you are forgiven. Here again, although forgiveness on one's part is of utmost importance, only a small part of what is required will be able to be redeemed.

For complete redemption, most of the accumulations of Negative Energy will have to be forgiven in another way.

There is a substance which has been qualified by God with redeeming, purifying properties, with Love and Forgiveness, and that Substance is Light, especially Violet (Purple) Light.

In John 8:12 Jesus states "I AM the Light of the world".

In I John 1:5 John writes "God is Light".

In Roman 13:12 Paul "Let us put on the armor of Light".

By adding the Fire element, we increase the Purifying Power of Light tremendously.

Ask you Indwelling I AM, your Indwelling Christ, to fill you and surround you with purifying, cleansing Violet Fire.

Then visualize and affirm that this Violet Fire is purifying and cleansing the whole area within you as well as around you.

This will go a long way toward forgiving and redeeming your accumulations of Negative Energy, thereby increasing the physical body's vibratory rate.

A number of the sayings concerning the overcoming of death and achieving Eternal Life involve believing in Jesus.

It's logical to conclude that believing in someone also involves believing in and following their teachings.

One very important teaching of Jesus with regard to conquering the last enemy was stated in John 8:51 when Jesus said "If a man keep my saying, he will never die".

I believe the most important saying of Jesus was in
John 10:30 when he said "I and the Father are one".

Jesus also said in John 14:10 "I AM in the Father, and the
Father is in me" which also suggests oneness.

But for real oneness, we have to merge with our
Indwelling I AM, our Indwelling Christ, and
actually become the Christ.
That's what Jesus did -- and -- when he became the
Christ, he overcame death.

One of the steps necessary to become the Christ and
overcome death is the perfecting of the physical
body, thereby raising it's vibratory rate and helping
it to regain its true state as a Spiritual Body.

Jesus and the Bible have given us a number of excellent
sayings in this regard.

In John 3:3 Jesus stated "Except a man be born again, he
cannot enter the kingdom of God".

In I Cor 15:44 Paul states "It is sown a natural body.
It is raised in Spiritual Body".

In I Cor 15:53 Paul states "The corruptible must put on
incorruption".

20

In Romans 12:2 Paul states "Be transformed by the
   renewing of your mind" .

In Philippians 2:5 Paul states "Let this mind be in you
   which was also in Christ Jesus".

In Genesis 1:27 it states "God created man (originally) in
   his own image, male and female".

In Mathew 5:48 Jesus states "Be ye Perfect even as your
   Father, which is in heaven, is Perfect".

In II Cor 3:18 Paul states "We all, beholding the glory of
   the Lord, are changed into the same image".

In John 7:24 Jesus states "Judge not according to
   appearances".

In Mark 8:34 Jesus states "Whoever will come after me, let
   him deny himself".

In II Cor 6:16 Paul states "Ye are a temple of the
   Living God".

Accordingly, to transform the physical body into a
   purified, perfected Spiritual Body, it is necessary to
   be born again by the renewing of our thoughts
   --and--in the process, we are to disregard
   appearances, make full use of our imagination, and

21

embrace the Truth by seeing ourselves as God created us in his image--a Perfect Spiritual Being in a Perfect Spiritual Body--and by blessing and thanking God that in Spirit and in Truth this is already so right now.

It's important to keep in mind that in John 14:24 Jesus states "The words which you hear are not mine but the Father's who sent me".

In John 14:10 Jesus states "The words that I speak unto you I speak not of myself, but the Father that dewelleth in me, he doeth the works".

So that when Jesus speaks, it is the I AM, the Christ, within speaking.

Of all Jesus' sayings, I believe the one that sums up best the way to Eternal Life is to be found in John 14:6 when Jesus stated "I AM the Way, the Truth, and the Life".

Also in John 14:6 Jesus stated "No one cometh unto the Father but by ME".

In John 17:3 Jesus states "This is Life Eternal that they know THEE, the only true GOD".

In John 3:17 Jesus states "God sent his SON into the world so that the world, through HIM, might be saved".

In Roman 8:11 Paul states "The Spirit of Jesus (his I AM, his Christ) raised up Jesus from the dead, and this same Spirit in you shall also quicken your mortal bodies.

In John 11:25 Jesus stated "He that believeth on ME, though he die, yet shall he live".

In John 11:25 Jesus stated "I AM the Resurrection and the Life".

In other words, your Indwelling I AM, your Indwelling Christ, is the Way, and the only Way, to the Resurrection and Eternal Life.

I AM the Way, the Truth, and the Life.
Regardless of appearances, in Spirit and in Truth, you are the I AM; you are the Christ, the Son/Daughter of God, God as an Individual, God Individualized.

In Genesis 1:27 it states "God created man in his own image, male and female".

In John 14:9 Jesus states "He who has seen me hath seen the Father".

23

In John 10:30 Jesus states "I and the Father are one".

In John 10:34 Jesus states "Ye are Gods".

In Mathew 28:18 Jesus states "All authority has been given to me in heaven and in earth".

To show that we are directly descended from God, Jesus said in Mathew 23:9 "Call no man upon the earth your Father, for one is your Father which is in heaven".

In Romans 8:16 Paul "The Spirit itself beareth witness with our Spirit that we are the children of God".

In Genesis 1:27 it states "God created man in his own image, male and female".

In John 3:6 Jesus "That which is born of Spirit is Spirit".

Therefore, having come forth from God, in Spirit and in Truth each one of us is a Spiritual Being, an I AM, a Christ.

In I John 2:17 John states "He that doeth the Will of God abideth forever".

Therefore, in achieving Eternal Life, the following saying of Jesus is of utmost importance when He states in Luke 22:42 "Not my will, but thine be done".

In John 8:32 Jesus states "You shall know the Truth, and the Truth shall make you free".

How shall we know the Truth?

In I John 2:27 John stated "You need not that any man teach you".

In John 16:13 & 14:17 Jesus "The Spirit of Truth, which dwelleth in you, shall guide you unto all Truth".

In Mathew 16:17 Jesus said "Flesh and blood has not revealed it unto you, but the Father which is in heaven".

In other words, the I AM, the Christ, within you will teach you the Truth, and show you the way to freedom and immortality.

Therefore, it is essential that you direct your attention within and listen so that you may hear the voice of your Indwelling I AM, you Indwelling Christ.

Be sure also to take the time to affirm with strong conviction the Truths and sayings outlined in this booklet during you daily periods of meditation.

And let's not forget what Jesus said in John 14:12.

"He that believeth on me, the works that I do shall he do also", and one of the things that Jesus did was to ascend into his Christ-Self, his I AM, and that's what we will have to do eventually.

To sum it all up:

You Indwelling I AM is the Way, the Truth, and the Life.

If overcoming death and achieving Eternal Life seems to be an impractical dream, keep the following in mind.

In Mathew 19:26 Jesus said
"With God (your Indwelling I AM), all things are possible".

In Proverbs 23:7 it states
"As a man thinketh in his heart, so is he".

In Mathew 8:13 Jesus stated
"It is done unto us as we believe".

In Mark 9:23 Jesus stated
"To them that believe, all things are possible".

Meditation

Beloved Indwelling I AM,
the image and likeness of God,
just like God,
God as an individual, God individualized,
my Real Divine Self.

Beloved Indwelling I AM,
I love you with all my heart, with all my soul,
        with all my strength.
I love you so.

Beloved Indwelling I AM,
All-Powerful, All-Knowing, Pure Divine Love,
anchored within my heart,
I love you so. I adore you.

Beloved Indwelling I AM,
I trust in you completely,
All-Powerful, All-Knowing I AM.
You know all things. You can do all things.
With you, all things are possible.
With you, nothing is impossible.

You can even perform miracles,
        Or what seems like miracles.

Beloved Indwelling I AM,
I trust in you completely.
I'm not concerned about anything.
I put all my affairs in your hands, and I just let go,
        and I remain totally at peace, completed relaxed.
I AM totally at peace, completely relaxed right now.
At all times I keep my thoughts peaceful and loving.
I trust in you completely, Beloved Indwelling I AM.

I call on the Law of Forgiveness.
I forgive everybody for all transgressions,
        for all mistakes of the past.
I forgive everything.
I also forgive myself.
I forgive and I AM forgiven.
I forgive and I AM forgiven.

Beloved Indwelling I AM,
I call on You to send your Blazing, Burning
        Violet Fire, burning away, removing
        everything that's not Perfect all around me,

your Blazing, Burning Violet Fire, burning away,
    removing everything that's not Perfect
    within every part of my body.
I bless You and thank You, Beloved Indwelling I AM,
    for sending your Blazing, Burning Violet Fire,
    burning away, removing everything that's
    not Perfect all around me as well as
    within every part of my body.

Beloved Indwelling I AM,
I call on You to send your Consuming Violet Fire,
    consuming everything that's not Perfect
    all around me,
your Consuming Violet Fire, consuming everything
    that's not Perfect within every part of my body.
I bless You and thank You, Beloved Indwelling I AM,
    for sending your Consuming Violet Fire,
    consuming everything that's not Perfect
    all around me as well as
    within every part of my body.

Beloved Indwelling I AM,
I call on You to send
    your Purifying, Cleansing Violet Fire,

purifying, cleansing everything that's not Perfect
all around me,
your Purifying, Cleansing Violet Fire, purifying,
cleansing everything that's not Perfect
within every part of my body.
I bless You and thank You, Beloved Indwelling I AM,
for sending your Purifying, Cleansing Violet Fire,
purifying, cleansing everything that's not Perfect
all around me as well as
within every part of my body.

Beloved Indwelling I AM,
I call on You to surround me, enfold me at all times in
your Impenetrable, Blazing White Light,
a Wall of Protection.
I bless You and thank You, Beloved Indwelling I AM,
for surrounding me, enfolding me at all times
in your Impenetrable, Blazing White Light,
a Wall of Protection.

And outside of this Impenetrable, Blazing White Light,
outside this Wall of Protection,
a Wall of Blue Flame, A Wall of Blue Fire,
as added Protection.

Beloved Indwelling I AM,
Thanks to You and thanks to your Unlimited Power,
     in Spirit and in Truth
     I AM a Perfect Spiritual Being
     in a Perfect Spiritual Body,
     a Young, Beautiful Spiritual Body,
     a Perfect Spiritual Body.
That's the way You created me in your image, and that's
     the way you continue to see me in your image,
     a Perfect Spiritual Being in a Perfect Spiritual Body,
     a Young, Beautiful Spiritual Body,
     a Perfect Spiritual Body.
Therefore, in Spirit and in Truth
     my body is now in Perfect condition.
I bless my Body.
I bless You and thank You , Beloved Indwelling I AM,
     for keeping my Body in Perfect condition.

Beloved Indwelling I AM,
I call on You to see to it that I ascend
     into your Divine Presence in this embodiment.
I bless You and thank You, Beloved Indwelling I AM,
     for seeing to it that I ascend
     into your Divine Presence in this embodiment.

31

And along with that I call on You to prepare me
	so that I will be able to ascend
	into your Divine Presence in this embodiment.
I bless you and thank you, Beloved Indwelling I AM,
	for preparing me so that I will be able to ascend
	into your Divine Presence in this embodiment.
Thanks to You and thanks to your Unlimited Power,
	as each day passes my ascension
	into your Divine Presence draws closer and closer.

Beloved Indwelling I AM,
I love you with all my heart.
I love You so.
I also love all of God's children, my brothers and sisters.
I love everybody.
I love everything,
But I love You most of all.

Beloved Indwelling I AM,
I trust in You completely.
I give myself to You unconditionally.
I surrender my mind, my body, my very life
	entirely into your hands, and I call on You
	to take complete control of my mind and my body.

I bless You and thank You, Beloved Indwelling I AM,
    for taking complete control
    of my mind and my body.

Therefore, In Spirit and in Truth You are now
    in complete control of my mind and my body
    so that of myself I do nothing.
You are with me always for You and I are One,
    absolutely and totally One.
You are anchored within my heart.
I bless You and thank You, Beloved Indwelling I AM,
    for your constant Indwelling Presence.

Yes, Beloved Indwelling I AM,
    of myself I do nothing.
It is You who do whatever is done, so that not my will
    but your Will is being done in all my affairs.

You are expressing yourself through me,
    through my mind and through my body.
You are expressing yourself through me as me,
    actually using my mind and my body
    as your very own
    so that whoever sees me is really seeing You.

I bless You and thank You, Beloved Indwelling I AM,
	for taking compete control
	of my mind and my body.

Beloved Jesus, Prince of Peace,
I love you with all my heart.
I love You so.
Help me ascend into my I AM Presence
	in this embodiment.
I bless You and thank you, Beloved Jesus,
	for helping me ascend into my I AM Presence
	in this embodiment.

Beloved Indwelling I AM,
I call on You to protect me with your Unlimited Power.
I bless You and thank You, Beloved Indwelling I AM,
	for protecting me with your Unlimited Power.

Beloved Indwelling I AM,
I call on You to guide me with your Infinite Wisdom,
	with your Infinite Knowledge.
I bless You and thank You, Beloved Indwelling I AM,
	for guiding me with your Infinite Wisdom,
	with your Infinite knowledge.

34

Therefore, Beloved Indwelling I AM,
        in Spirit and in Truth
        you are guiding me with your Infinite Wisdom,
        with your Infinite Knowledge,
        and I hear your voice.
I hear your voice.
I hear your voice.
Beloved Indwelling I AM---I AM---I AM

NOTES

NOTES

NOTES

NOTES

NOTES

NOTES

NOTES

NOTES

NOTES

NOTES

ISBN 1-41205081-2

9 781412 050814